Survival in the Arctic

Explorer Challenge

Find out what the hare is looking for ...

OXFORD
UNIVERSITY PRESS

It was snowing. Dad was taking the children out to play on their sledges.

"It's very, very cold," said Dad. "You need to wrap up. Go back and put on lots of warm clothes and your thick coats."

"My boots are so hard to take off," said Chip, as he ran upstairs. "I'm keeping them on."

"So am I," said Biff.

Chip put on lots of layers of clothes and went
into Biff's room. Biff had put on lots of warm
clothes, too. At that moment, the key glowed.

The key took them to the Arctic in Canada.
All around them were fir trees covered in snow.
"I'm glad we put on warm clothes," said Biff.

Just then, they heard someone calling for help.
"Someone's in trouble," said Chip.
In the distance they saw a girl waving. "Will
you help me?" she called.

The girl's name was Kimi.

"We have had an accident," she said. "Our snowmobile hit a hidden tree stump. My twin brother, Kitchi, is in trouble. His leg is trapped."

"I'm not hurt," said Kitchi, "but I can't pull my leg out. We need some help. Kimi isn't strong enough to lift the snowmobile up on her own."

Chip had an idea. "If we get some thick branches, maybe we can tip the snowmobile over," he said.

"That will work," said Kitchi.

They found some heavy branches to lift the snowmobile and Kitchi pulled his leg free.

"We're stuck," said Kitchi. "When we don't come home, our parents will know something is wrong and send help. But help may not get here until tomorrow."

"Don't you have a mobile phone?" asked Biff.
"Yes, we do," said Kitchi, "but I forgot to charge it."
"That's a big mistake to make in the Arctic," said Kimi, "so we're stuck!"

"We'll just have to make a shelter and keep warm until help arrives," said Kitchi.

"Er ... you mean we're going to have to spend the night out here?" gasped Biff.

"Let's hope the key glows first," whispered Chip.

Kimi looked at the twins. "We've slept out all
night before," she said. "But you need proper
clothes to keep you warm."

She went to the sled and found coats and gloves.

"We carry spare clothes," she said, "in case we
get wet. Put these on over your coats."

Kitchi took an axe and a saw out of the sled.
"We need lots of wood," he said.

Biff and Chip collected wood for the fire. Kimi
began to build the shelter. She fixed a long pole
between some trees and rested more poles against it.

"The back of the shelter must be against the
wind," she said.

Suddenly a cascade of snow fell on Chip's head.
Everyone laughed.

"Sorry!" said Kitchi. "But that's what happens
if you stand under a tree covered in snow!"

Kitchi dug up stones to put a fire on.

"We need to work fast," said Kitchi. "It will get dark soon. We need to have plenty of firewood to keep the fire burning all night."

Kimi melted some snow to make a hot drink. "Don't forget, it is important to drink a lot," she told them.

Kitchi grilled some fish on a metal grill. "We caught the fish this morning in the frozen lake," he said. "We were on our way home from the fishing trip when the sled turned over."

They settled down for the night.

"Try to get some sleep," said Kimi.

Later, Biff heard something snorting outside the shelter. She was scared. "Kitchi! Kimi!" she whispered. "There's a bear outside!"

"It's only a moose," said Kitchi.

He threw a log on to the fire. A shower of sparks
flew up and the moose ran away.

"Come and see this," said Kitchi.

They went out of the shelter and he pointed up at the sky. "The moose did us a good turn," he said. "Because of him, we can see something amazing. Look!"

Biff and Chip gasped. Above them were streaks of green light that hung like a brightly coloured curtain across the sky.

"These are the Northern Lights," said Kitchi.

"Wow! It's just beautiful," gasped Chip.
"Why does it happen?"

"You had better look it up on the Internet,"
said Kimi.

The next morning, Kitchi got the fire to make thick white smoke. A few minutes later, the rescue helicopter appeared.

"Rescue!" said Kitchi.

Just then the key glowed.

"What an adventure!" said Biff. "Now I know what it's like to be really cold."

"I'm glad we've got warm beds to sleep in tonight," said Chip.

In the garden, Chip shook the tree that Dad was standing under. Snow cascaded down on Dad's head.

The children laughed.

"Hey!" yelled Dad.

"Sorry, Dad!" said Chip. "But that's what happens if you stand under a tree covered in snow."

Retell the Story

Look at the pictures and retell the story in your own words.

Look Back, Explorers

Where did the magic key take Biff and Chip?

How did they build a shelter?

How do you think Chip felt when the snow landed on his head?

What questions would you like to ask Kimi and Kitchi about surviving for a night in the Arctic?

When Chip shook the tree, snow *cascaded* down on Dad's head. What does *cascaded* mean?

Did you find out what the hare was looking for?

Explorer Challenge: food – it digs up moss to eat (page 15)

What's Next, Explorers?

Now you've read about Biff and Chip's night surviving in the Arctic, find out what people, plants and animals need to survive …

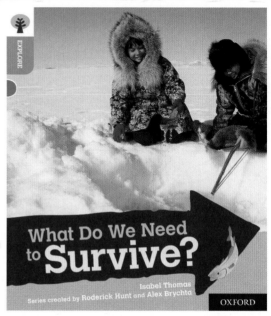

What Do We Need to Survive?

Isabel Thomas
Series created by Roderick Hunt and Alex Brychta

OXFORD

Explorer Challenge
for *What Do We Need to Survive?*

Find out how this beetle survives in a desert …